SOURCE TO MOUTH

BRANDON KRIEG

SOURCE TO MOUTH

BRANDON KRIEG

NEW MICHIGAN PRESS
TUCSON, ARIZONA

NEW MICHIGAN PRESS
DEPT OF ENGLISH, P. O. BOX 210067
UNIVERSITY OF ARIZONA
TUCSON, AZ 85721-0067

<http://newmichiganpress.com/nmp>

Orders and queries to nmp@thediagram.com.

Copyright © 2012 by Brandon Krieg.
All rights reserved.

ISBN 978-1-934832-39-4. FIRST PRINTING.

Printed in the United States of America.

Interior design by Ander Monson.

Cover image and design by Laura Mackin and Seth Nelson.

CONTENTS

I, Inc. 1
Fallen Empire's Tiny Chemical Sun 8
Tired of Explaining Seasons to the Sun, 9
Inversion Among the Fish Counters at Bonneville
   Dam 12
Note from the Romans 14
Speck 16
November 18
Calling 19
Note from the Etruscans 20
October 21
Preserve 22
After Hopkins 24
Magus 25
Case Study 26
Note from Pergamon 27
A Dish of Roman Nails 28
A Door 29
The Cloisters 30
Borromini's Ceiling at San Carlo 31
Sundress 32
Indivisible 33
Note from an Ascendant Sect 34
Conditions of Blood 35

The End of Metaphor   36
Fishing Rock   39
Compass   40
Levels   41
Invasives   42
Out at the Root   45

Acknowledgments   47

For my parents

I, INC.

I incorporate gneiss and coal and
    long-threaded moss
    and fruits and grains
and esculent roots, a gravity dam
    550 feet high on this
    the continent's steepest
river machine, with 13 other dams, a system
    of locks and
ladders for commerce, continuance

of species, twin
cooling towers of a data-center
    for the world's most powerful
search engine, installed at the site of a lost
    Babel where first
    peoples converged
in that universal language: trade, night-spearing

of salmon by torchlight
    lost (men's faces aflash
    in archives), expressionist
    petroglyphs eerily
    contemporary, photographed
by professors before
    the big sink, I incorporate

with irrigation ditches, thousands
    of gridded miles
of piping, hoses, scaffolding for sprinklers,
    insecticide banners
    over alfalfa terraces greenshining to the edge
    of the glacier-cut gorge,

and on the ridges:
white windmills, futurist
    crosses, revivalist
architecture of potato magnates, societies
    for the preservation of automatic, semi-automatic,
    Gun Hill, Gun River, without judgment—
that sucked candy—I incorporate

the leaden
    groundwater under
firing range and echoing
factory, the capful of phosphates,
    Chicago River run backward
    to Mississippi, algae clotting
the Gulf's left ventricle, plumes of oil filmed
    by unmanned cameras
    designed to sustain
unearthly pressure, ingenious inhibitors
    of serotonin reuptake
present from sewage in measurable amounts
    in the Great Lakes,
    and calm

as the not-I appears, I incorporate
the not-I,

the talkers
in headsets talking to no one present,
Bach and baseball and
    tobacco stocks ticking, the screen-lit
    lotuseating faces staring,
clicking—disgust me, and I incorporate them
    with disappearing

bees, defense drones
undetectable except
    by ordnance flowering
    skull, sternum, uterus, I am born
    at many removes
from Thoreau, who paused to notice
    the thickness of surface ice,

and, tormented
by his still form in the hut doorway,
sun on skin, outside time, I incorporate it and it binds
    the mettle in my blood,
    the compound sinking
to my feet—impossibly heavy, I drive them

into mountains topped with blinking
towers, ziggurated by
    logging roads, in motley
    of clear-cuts and
necklaced with triple-stranded cables whose buzzing
sounds like rain, and up there
    walking the ancient

Cascade Volcanic Arc, I incorporate
the green company of grunts
    on leave in sunburned skulls, who go
    silent posing
on a high promontory—premonitions
    of Hindu Kush—they frighten me
    with politeness
on the trail, acne, and large vulnerable ears,
I could clap their shoulders, clasp them, pretend to

spar as with my brothers,
but, helpless to keep them
    for their families' sakes
    from disappearing
into the photograph's digital veil, can only
    incorporate them as I must
    these actors charging the hill
    on a screen in a window
I walk under later, many rooms are lit this way,
the allegory literalized, and I am outside

in another cave
of streetlights flicking on under cameras,
I pass through these and incorporate their recordings of me
      into that Gordian nerve-net
      of me not recorded, firing
      charges down too many
      forks to be
      reliably
      modeled, the loops
      of its feedback with external
stimuli so intricately innested, a representation

of them would curve its outer ring
      through the Oort,
      and I must go farther,
      into imagined futures, incorporate
cornstalks 12 feet high with black leaves modified
by photosynthetic silicates for 90% efficiency of capture
      and acorn-sized kernels,
      they are beautiful if not yet
      realized, and I am afraid
of them, utterly, as I was in Chicago homesick

for Trask and Kilchis, Siletz and Nestucca, and found,
at the Eastern end of Pratt Street where it abuts the Lake,
      frozen corpses of
      Chinook Salmon
washed up like grotesques out of my memory—
transplants are everywhere, translations of
translations, no place embodies itself, all

overlap, and so I
incorporate them, unifying
them in one brand,
    Brandon, meaning
    from a flaming hill
as claimed by a bookmark given me when young—
    I place it in the book of grass
and the book catches fire and illuminates
    the undersides of clouds,
    an advertisement like the orange GE
glowing on a building in Midtown
    seen by the lovers
    naked in infinite
    regress of two walls of hotel-room mirrors,

and, full disclosure: it was I positioned against her
    in the mirrors' smallest frame,
feeling I lived in invisible abstract cornucopia diminishment
    of frame within frame where
only images propagate—invincible-distant
as the acronym haloes guarding Mannahatta's skyline—

corporations are all.

Resist or acquiesce, I incorporate
their paltry specializations into this brand
    whose acronym is every star in the night sky,
    and in the day sky too,
    for though it is invisible, it is nevertheless
    present, totalizing, undemocratic
as every corporation aspires to be,

    and, reader far hence,
face lit by a little held charge, a little water's motion,
    a million-stranded rope of sand,
all of my swindling and evasion is for our certain merger,
    for I am corrupt as every other,
    and you must absorb my assets

as I have absorbed this
    broadcast image
from Stalin's Ukrainian famine—the infant automaton
    in the street still nursing on
    its starved dead mother.

Swallow me and go.
I do not wait for you I am in you already.
There is commerce between us.

FALLEN EMPIRE'S TINY CHEMICAL SUN

Timberline reached,
I dig old snow
to heat on a tin
East German folding stove;
add jasmine tea—
Sunflower Brand,
Fujian Province—
to the pot; mark
the fuel disk's origin:
Chemische Fabrik
Westeregeln;
read the tea tin's
proclamation: People's
Republic; see far
Seattle in smog gone
sunset-molten;
savor the lees.

TIRED OF EXPLAINING SEASONS TO THE SUN,

I on the mountain descended
    below the clouds, to overturn loose slates
on the black stream's rubble bottom.

I picked from the first slate an elegant utterance,
    a caddisfly's woven pebble cone
    stitched with nearly invisible spicules
    to its obscure stone roof,
and peeled the pebble cone to see

    the appalled pupa
filtering specks of plant-matter
into pulpy, papery wings,
    to smuggle them clumsily
    to the stream's surface someday

(to float in total vulnerability
to cutthroat trout, common sparrows,
streamside webs), waiting for the sun to dry them

that it might clobber and climb a mate
    in air, completing its pattern no closer to the sun
    than tips of shoreline scrub;

    but in peeling, I
    split the soft wing-sac
    with a barbed thumb.

There was no repairing
>	the plucked one unpearling
in my palm, so I begged the flashing trout-mouths
return this

and climbed a rise above the stream scooped sheer
>	by an eddy's clockwise coil,
>	parted thick weeds, and peered
into the coil's center:

a thousand tinier spindles of spring-water unwound
long strands of silt,
>	and muscular shapes, suspended
against the loose ends, flicked livid tails
>	over a seam of bluish alluvium.

>	I dripped the sticky pupa
>	from thumb-tip
>	into stream's pupil.

The mouths blinked wildly,
clouds broke behind me, making the water mirror
>	my crouching form, revealing the sun
>	crouching over me.

I turned, scrambled back from the rise, and was
    snared by a strand of nettles;
    barbed weed split my lip,
    ground knocked the seasons out of me,
and leaves disguised as never fallen cried

return this return this.

INVERSION AMONG THE FISH COUNTERS
AT BONNEVILLE DAM

I could count seven hundred salmon flashes in an hour
while watching in that falling wall of water
the triumph of Caesar, red as Capitoline Jupiter,

not long before he was murdered and deified. Some still leave,
it's said, flowers in the forum where his tomb is thought to be.
Nevermind. I was a Classics major home from the university

with a nervous disorder, was told a repetitive task
might take my mind off Rome's decline. I sat before a glass
viewing window and counted, in their spawning masks—

hook-jawed, severe—male Chinook returning.
Joe Garrison sat in the other folding chair, burning
as he said, his Indian half with a flask, and earning

nearly twice my wage for the more difficult-to-spot hens.
"What's your other half, Joe?" I asked. "Half salmon,"
he said, "what's yours?" I said: "Imperial Roman."

He laughed. "The best gladiators were Colville Indians," he said,
"They learned by spearing salmon to spear a man dead
at thirty yards, from a speeding El Camino's bed."

I laughed hard. Then wanting to reach him these words
formed by inversion before I could check them. We both heard:
"To kill a man, kill his salmon—that's what the Romans learned."

NOTE FROM THE ROMANS

Punch eyeholes in your helmets
and be skulled messengers
    of death. A simple cage
is good to hold the most grotesque

creatures on display. Perfect the placement
of pebble-sized mosaic tiles
    and you will be kept

from growing finned tails and slipping
into irreversible water; you will build a bridge

high enough to make the sky
flow under it
    like a parade of prisoners.

Still, you may be awakened by a sound
of jugs pouring over stones.

The cages will be wet but empty,
the winds seem heated by the faraway

clapping of burst men's mouths
like cod-mouths grasping
                at strange light.

And if the same light
                    should seem to fall
from the bridge at night, making it shiver

in the forward ripples of the river,
cover, if you can,
                    your lidless eyes.

SPECK

My father appears, creased
to sell machines, whose ion beams
detect, on polished silicon disks,
defective circuit memory.

He opens his briefcase to show
a darkened salmon.
It's been polished so often
it has hardened like a totem.
It is stranger than Leviathan.
It is formed of our Lord Doubt.

When he is alone,
my father takes it out
and sets it on the hotel bed.
This proves to him he had a son
who shied from the insistence of the depths.

And the father took the creaking pole,
and pulled against the beast with jagged grin,
and shrapnel up and down its skin,
and bottles breaking up its belly,
whose slime is saccharine and scent of lilies,
whose nostrils blind its eyes with smoke,
who clacks like keyboards fin to finish,
whose half-life shames our hopes.

And our Lord Doubt spoke:
Behold: you cannot see him he is probable.
Behold: you cannot see him he is wave.
Lay thy approximation against him;
remember the battle.

My father tells me, *Haul this memory*
through every city
and stuff its mouth with votive money,
it has become too heavy.
But he is trapped inside of it
with me: an egg within an egg within an egg.

Inside, Lord,
I feel your speck of silicate.

NOVEMBER

Childwise vision
of a coho thrashing in thin floodwater blankets
on a black road.

Enraged with milt, it slithers over asphalt;
it will not reach the redd;
it will not pass the code
that maps from source to mouth its fluent god.

Yet I return to its
struggle ditch-ward to spawn alone
on the sharp, damp rocks.

This is where I was born.

CALLING

I could go credulous, could call
diminished sixths from the blanching chips
of a mouse's skull;

could take the rushes cased in ice
slow, slow, until the cases' tonic cracking
was fast below in nets of roots;

could loud, like the jay, rip shreds
of moss, richly dropletted, to incorporate
my vanishing;

could swell with the creek to cull
scribbled commandments from lowest branches—
transient, yet
influencing the effluence;

could follow in deep leaf-muck
creek's meandering, and find unlooked-for ferns'
green deafening. I sat then,

incredulous, in colors beyond calling, sat
until I picked from the din the heron's eye
that transforms

low fish-bones into long, silent flight.

NOTE FROM THE ETRUSCANS

When you are finally alone, the canopy of your wings
will drape over you, the stream will run through
the comb of your bones without straightening,
and the shadows of your breasts will be kept in shallow bowls.

If you missed the path where the seedpods stop rattling,
your necklace will have to be slipped off and lost
before you can wade into the silence

of a simple handle dropped in a field,
before you can know a wheel turned on its side
is a round of contentment to confound the clouds.

Even then you will find your eyes are stylized olives
painted on a slate, that have never actually opened,
and your mouth opened to sing is full of seeds rattling.
Then your whole body will slip through your ring.

OCTOBER
for John Keats and Nick Drake

Autumnals overheard
in the next room, I have passed the place
where you turned back.

The loaded apple boughs are there,
color unchanging; a sound repeats

your second grace forever.
I drive on, into late corn, find everywhere
wide paths cut for cables

that feed the alien screens.
On one screen I saw shining husks rustle

with your words in the chill
celibacy that has crept backward
over your lives. This room is smallest.

The corn of Ruth, even, is gone.

PRESERVE

A tall animal has printed the snow drift
on this pond's ice roof.
Incautious to the risk of falling through,
it has crossed. Emerson

assured a version of me more integral
awaits my determination to meet it
in woods. He uses me

to meet himself in woods in me.
On the shoreline, through shafts in the snow crust:
cleft hoofprints, frail blue.

Deer or devil this creature walks
ungingerly, drops scat freely, peels long strips
of bark from oldest trees, and the trace
its walking makes—doubling and redoubling,
impossible to follow—makes
its way its way.

I stand in dense saplings the hoof prints have split
to cross the pond. Will I find I wait for me
on that other side, or find Emerson only
an echo

diminished to this preserve?
Such a thin roof of ice upholds such wondering.
It shakes and crazes in the human thunders
of planes in descent to O'Hare.

I stand out under the evaporating banners
of others' journeys—earth is rapidly less than actual
size.

Trace I read in the snow, you are wise.
I must be otherwise.

AFTER HOPKINS

Indivisible I divine
    in leaf's veins, lung's blood,
        floodplain and feathered cloud,
where the all ails, avail.

We've summoned by reduction
    the valenced none, digressed,
        through manias of distinction,
out of reverence, are undeceived

and undone. Therefore, repair.
    Let mountain and meteorite
        accord in scale, write in alleles
aves in human and bacterium alike.

Let us learn to lean again
    on the awe-obstinate phrase,
        like that poor priest who fused
the disparate trout spots,

        cloud colors, into one praise.

MAGUS

I pick the dandelion's
pointillist eye, blow it blind.

One astral capsule
fastens a spider's zodiac.

The spider, in
concentric meditation,

despite this
interpolation, is

undivided.
I am guided.

CASE STUDY

In the new buildings
are the old buildings;

in the old buildings
are the felled forests;

in the felled forests
are the forgotten verses;

in the forgotten verses
are the simple arrows

in glass cases
in the new buildings.

NOTE FROM PERGAMON

The horses have trampled their legs to rubble;
the archer's hand floats free of his body at last.

Our glacial breasts have slipped down the precipice;
rain softened our genitals to sorrowful marshland.

From our geometries, chimeras overcoming
earth; serpents nurse on the grease of our axles.

Do not pity us, passenger on this
altar ship. You too are steered by a torso

whose thoughts are smoke of sacrifices.

A DISH OF ROMAN NAILS

A clear glass dish of imperial noise;
of wood-and-plaster-wept ironic tears;
stripped pinnets of the augurs' foiled ploys;
creaking eyelashes of the brothel boys;
and prisoners' scratched-out years.

Who will return the spiders' obelisks,
re-order the teeth of the just decree,
discover again the geometers' styluses,
and calibrate the pleasure and the risk
of their breakneck traceries?

A nest of erections come to nothing,
monotonous notes of pounded praise,
full of the silence of—gravely opening
to witness the burdened elephant triumphing—
a thousand dismantled doorways.

A DOOR

Cities, streets, narrow to a door.
When you will arrive at it, how
it will transform what comes before
remains obscure. This is sure: it is

creaking near. The threshold
approaches to mute your feet
even as you sleep. I woke

in many cities: in Brooklyn woke
to lightning revealing a plot
of back-lot cornstalks: tall

as any door I'd ever seen.
I felt it seal the air. I could wake
all over earth, but I could not
hide this knock anywhere.

THE CLOISTERS

Removed from pilgrimage routes,
reassembled across an ocean,
these arches once enclosed the spirit's orders
until death, and housed the bones.

Their placement now reflects, however mitigated
by curators' antiseptic fingers, a magnate's preference—
the rigors of the cross have been dispensed with,
and windows added facing the summer Hudson.

The Sunday crowd looks out, it shuffles through
to see elsewhere the apse, the tapestries kept dark
preserving priceless gilts of cryptic dukes.
A dissected narwhale's horn offers proof
of the existence of the unicorn.

But linger under the rectilinear skylight
that protects from open air these courtyard walls,
and no fleshed-out relic of the Word could seem enough
to take the walls again as limits of a life.

Instead a vision comes, of the vast pleasures left
to those freed from laying prayerful bedrock,
and in it, a Rockefeller sadly having his choice
of another stone head, in the purchasable world.

BORROMINI'S CEILING AT SAN CARLO

Oh
vowel around
elliptical lip, oh fill
elongated lozenge with
feathered light, oh brightly
oscillating weather of tessel-
lations, refract shadowy,
collapse constantly, oh
glory me, sun-stun-
ning dove-
hive.

SUNDRESS

This house crouches
under the others' porches.
Its driftwood-gray Victorian

scrollwork is ridiculous
when glimpsed in the total ambush
of rhododendron.

In the door, a narrow window is
hung for blind with a tie-dyed
dress, yellowish,

its sleeves pinned in alleluia position
to the frame's interior. The fashion
is forty years dead,

yet sunlight has so inhabited
the space hips belly and breasts once
lent dimension,

the dress seems to have been
hung here because
sunlight is

the size its wearer was.

INDIVISIBLE

She had been split already—twin
emerging after
an assertive sister;

split again
when one ear went dim
in a childhood disease;

split by early work,
her hands sweeping up
the bones bit clean by truckers
in the nightclub her father owned;

split by a church
that hung the naked beauty on the cross
and demanded that she cover up her knees.

Her growth was a meiosis reversed,
sloughing unnecessary halves

to consolidate the germ. She became
indivisible, the smallest nested doll

inside the parent shell
of a Dakota sky,

and then I split her
with my cries.

NOTE FROM AN ASCENDANT SECT

We were told to plant nothing on the cliffs,
though no angel landed there ever.
When we went for water, some heard bleeding

behind the wall. Some saw the fluid coil
of the ram's horn repeated in the field's snakes,
and buried their vision in furrows—later, flowers

ensnared the corn. But we couldn't hide
our nakedness from ourselves,
or stop feeling our flesh as a curtain

draping the eyes of our children.
We couldn't stop hearing wings
of skin descending like trickles of light

and bright rays of water. A trail of keys
led the prophet to our corner of earth,
though he left us suddenly, finding no

locked chests to open. Often, two of us
were met coming back from the cliffs
with an upwelling secret.

CONDITIONS OF BLOOD

Long before Joverape and virginbirth, the sea
rubbed fresh genitals against continents
climaxing in the mineral
conditions of
blood,

fell shivering back into clitoral cloud-hood:
lightning overloading its
synapses—proto-
bacterial

life!

Compulsion without remedy.

THE END OF METAPHOR

1.

This godawful clod of man
    with eyeglasses warped
as sea-relinquished bottleglass,

by which he tracks his blessed dog
where the surf shrinks, has turned
    and waits for me, his hand

juggling free of weed strands
    a thing he gives to me:
That's a rare find—angel wings!

which is a white mussel shell
opened, pinioned
        to him as

the terrible anomalies
shrieking down
heaven.

It crumbles in the hinge of my outstretched
mind.
They're usually broken up;

        find another if you're lucky.

2.

Picking through strangulated kelp,
I find the buried bulb
at coil's end.

Stretch the unreal length straight out—
    livid scourge!
        monstrous sperm!

O unlikeness.

Pick through
    the mossy beards stripped
from prophets, washed

ashore here—where
are your microbial lips, Pythagoras?
Pick apart green strands

and find the sand flea's throne:
a trail of bubbles going deeper,
                my love says,

kissed by unlikeness.

3.

That angel-winged sand flea
Giordano Bruno,
      that mutation stricken,

no sandgrain glinting has yet
escaped his mnemonic,
      who evaporated

at the stake, now beads
a hundredfold
on the oils

of a tern's lost under-down tuft:
image that has nothing to do
      with Argus,

that watches over my life.

FISHING ROCK

Black monolith annealed of numberless obsidian dice
waiting to be worn free, rolled by wave fingers
without tally—

moon wins—

aloof in remote gravity, yet formed
of the same force

that melded these billion particulars
into an awe-shape:

disks of pumice   black dice

no bones   all vaporized

no delicate inlines to suggest the muscular outlines
that once shot through sea like a shower of arrows—

sun the archer—

only a gray tufa-like slab crowning the black rock:
spolia of an empire, fossil-less
as the moon.

The sun stops first at its altar.

COMPASS

Mussels cluster on black rocks like magnetic shavings.

God my compass
with many centers and no circumference,
I am lost

in you since I relinquished
sex my pole star—

the long, red needle-beaks pry
the black shells open

to thrill flesh, but you are love
without proof or precedent, therefore:

Love, Augustine

                              Down here!
love is usage.

LEVELS

Every pit high in the cliff's terraces lives
on the sea's excesses—
sculpins, anemones, small crabs the color of stone

shift and twitch in shallow cragpools,
unaware worlds
upon worlds enfold their stratospheres of foam:

star-freaked domes, bald thrall moons
that sway
disturbances in remote elements:

the tidal jets and sprays, for instance,
refreshing these
oases of gill and claw that also fill the dead

crabs' littered, picked-clean
headpieces
with reflections of such wide

miniscule skies.

INVASIVES

High tide pressed me
up into
    the yellow, invasive
Scotch broom

whose roots hold fast this
crumbling cliff.

Against root-give, I clung
    ever more urgently to the *still,
small voice*—whose seeds

blew into me from 19c fields—
watching tankers drag

coal hillsides, tourist districts, shining decks
of cars past
    distant peaks,

and since this tide would not
retreat,
    cut a hard path up the cliff,
made my way through vacationers

sauntering the green of a fin de siècle
fort. Where genteel, sympathetic

        murder was taught,
in haphazard rows,
children at art camp lounged with ice creams,

laughing avidly. There must be a real
higher or harder
than this, I said,

and took the trail up to a bluff overlooking
international waters,

        walked the rim of the impregnable
        concrete walls of the abandoned

gun emplacements. This is a place, finally,

nothing can invade,
I thought—admiring

        the Mayan-monumentality
        stripped

of phony deity—
I can build hard
        apprehension here.

Up a narrow ladder, I climbed
    into the watchtower,

shut the iron visor, and
    sat in ammonia-smelling dark

where *deep* and *calm* and *perpetual*
could never take.

Then Japanese fire-balloons
        floated elegantly

past the long-range guns in this afterimage
of a state-park plaque, touching down

70 years ago
    in Montana forests, igniting
    a recent candidate's promise

of colonies on the moon.

OUT AT THE ROOT

Shore pine on the sea cliff,
perennial axletree on which
stars wheel— waves of the highest

high tide have half-unearthed
its hold. The intricate rootwork
that like sight of the covenant's ark

none should know, hangs exposed:
rainwashed, rope-thick roots scaffold
the vacancy where cliff was, and ends

of dangling rootlets, thread-thin,
pulse droplets like rosaries broken
continually. The upper canopy un-greens

needle by needle; the low notched
branch-ends interlock to gnash
in wind. Even its sudden hush is a harsh

suspension between constellation's cog
and log undressed by waves, ring by ring.
The immanence of no returning

deity inheres in its last distress.
It is a high unblessed separateness,
at last. At last, it is relentless.

ACKNOWLEDGMENTS

Grateful acknowledgment is due to the editors of the journals where versions of some of these poems first appeared:

32 Poems: "Sundress."
American Letters and Commentary: "A Door."
Borderlands: Texas Poetry Review: "Borromini's Ceiling at San Carlo."
Cincinnati Review: "Note from Pergamon."
Commonweal: "After Hopkins," "Out at the Root."
Conjunctions (Web): "I, Inc."
CutBank: "The End of Metaphor."
DIAGRAM: "Invasives."
Faultline: "Fallen Empire's Tiny Chemical Sun."
The Iowa Review: "Note from an Ascendant Sect," "Note from the Etruscans."
The Journal: "Magus."
Mare Nostrum: "A Dish of Roman Nails."
Minnetonka Review: "Inversion among the Fish Counters at Bonneville Dam," "The Cloisters."
North American Review: "Preserve."
North Dakota Quarterly: "Speck."
Notre Dame Review: "Levels."
Portland Review: "Note from the Romans."
Roanoke Review: "Indivisible."
Seneca Review: "Case Study," "Tired of Explaining Seasons to the Sun."

Shenandoah: "Calling."
The Spoon River Poetry Review: "November."

"Compass," "Conditions of Blood," and "Fishing Rock" were published in a dialogue with poems by T. Zachary Cotler in *Likestarlings*.

COLOPHON

Text is set in a digital version of Jenson, designed by Robert Slimbach in 1996, and based on the work of punchcutter, printer, and publisher Nicolas Jenson.

BRANDON KRIEG grew up in Tualatin, OR and studied at Cornell University, The University of Washington, and Western Michigan University. His poems have appeared in *The Iowa Review*, *Web Conjunctions*, *Shenandoah*, and many other journals. He is a founding editor of *The Winter Anthology* and an associate editor of *Poetry Northwest*. He lives in Kalamazoo with his wife, Colleen O'Brien.

NEW MICHIGAN PRESS, based in Tucson, Arizona, prints poetry and prose chapbooks, especially work that transcends traditional genre. Together with DIAGRAM, NMP sponsors a yearly chapbook competition.

DIAGRAM, a journal of text, art, and schematic, is published bimonthly at THEDIAGRAM.COM. Periodic print anthologies are available from the New Michigan Press at NEWMICHIGANPRESS.COM/NMP.

www.ingramcontent.com/pod-product-compliance
Lightning Source LLC
Chambersburg PA
CBHW031503040426
42444CB00007B/1193